# 7 DAYS TO A MAGICKAL NEW YOU

# 7 DAYS TO A MAGICKAL NEW YOU

Fiona Horne

Thorsons

Thorsons
An Imprint of HarperCollins*Publishers*
77–85 Fulham Palace Road, Hammersmith, London W6 8JB

The Thorsons website address is: www.thorsons.com

Published by Thorsons 2001

1 3 5 7 9 8 6 4 2

© Fiona Horne 2001

Fiona Horne asserts the moral right to be
identified as the author of this work

A catalogue record for this book is available from the British Library

ISBN 0 00 712346 9

Printed and bound in Great Britain by
Martins the Printers Limited, Berwick-upon-Tweed

# contents

# Blessed Be

My heartfelt thanks and love go to:
Shelli-Anne Couch, Kate Nobelius, Louise McNamara,
Karen Kreiger, Megan Slyfield, Mum and Dad, Clint
Bizzell, Cyndi Puertas, Krista Vendy, Lydia Visintin, Phyllis
Curott, Dylan Masson, Erika Schulz, Yelba Quinn, Bill
Beattie, Franklin and Mauritzio Winkler, Simone and
Zoya at dog-eared designs, Gene, Jeff Zaleski and ... you!

# A MAGICKAL MAKEOVER

**This book is a guide to giving yourself a magickal makeover in just one week. In this short period of time you can unveil your hidden powers, fire up your focus, and launch into the rest of your life in an empowered and vibrant way!**

Are you drawn to the color and creativity of Witchcraft, but are not sure about being an actual Witch? The methods in this book are adapted from powerful Witchcraft practices but presented in such a way that an absolute "newbie" can easily and successfully enjoy them. Or perhaps you have been a practicing Witch for a while, but you've hit a bit of a plateau in your powers and you'd like to rev them up a bit – then this book is for you too.

By giving yourself a magickal makeover you are empowering yourself in a pure and unique way. When you feel charged and confident, a lot of problems will seem to evaporate. When you are connected to the deep wise self that lies within, the outside world is easier to navigate. Negative thought and behavioral patterns shift and new ways of being are enlightened.

If you really want to enhance your magickal self, taking a week off work or other commitments is certainly the way to do it. However, if your job, family, or boyfriend commitments just can't be budged for the moment, then each day or a selection of days can be undertaken, tailored to your specific requirements.

But remember, whether you spend a day or a week
on your makeover it requires dedication! You're not
taking a holiday. Some of the work you'll undertake won't
be easy (though a lot of it will be a breeze) – but the
results will be well worth the effort!

The ultimate aim of the week is to create an
enchanted sense of self. The whole experience should
be approached with a sense of fun and adventure.
Also, be aware that the activities described are intended
to inspire you. You can follow everything to the letter
if you want, but I always emphasize that the most
magickal experiences are usually the ones that you
create yourself. So don't be afraid to experiment and
expand on the suggestions to fulfil your desires.

Try to time your week around the waxing and full moon (supercharged times to do magick of any sort). However, even though there are rituals that are enhanced by these phases, it's certainly not essential. By focusing properly you can make this week very potent, regardless of what the moon is doing.

You will be spending a lot of the week alone, and you need to find somewhere private where you can perform your magickal work without interruption. I would suggest stocking up the fridge and pantry with lots of fresh, nutritious foods – however, this isn't a diet, so don't plan to double your magickal week with a weight loss program.

It will only be distracting and, anyway, part of what you are doing here is rising above society's pre-conceived notions of appropriate appearances and behavior to accept how amazing you are unconditionally. Fresh, simple foods will allow easy digestion and provide the brain and body with lots of nutrients, which will help you work magick more effectively.

Have a good read through this book and make a list of everything you'll need (herbs and oils for the spells and potions, candles, books etc.) and try to stock up on all these at the start. Then the only time you'll need to leave your space is to perform one or two of the suggested rituals and to go for a nice walk in a park, forest, or along the beach. Also, remember to turn off your cell phone and take the telephone off the hook when you don't want to be disturbed!

You should also really familiarize yourself with the work you intend to undertake before you start – even run through the planned activities in your head the day before. The key to great magickal transformation is focus and intent – if you are spending the day worrying that you're not doing it right, that you've forgotten something, or if you are in any other way distracted, you won't get the results you want.

✳ **NOTE:** *If you have flicked through this book and decide to just do, for example, Wednesday, I suggest you read the whole book from start to finish before you focus on your specific day choice. There are lots of tips and hints throughout the book that you should familiarize yourself with before you start.*

## A MAGICKAL SHOPPING LIST

The following is a general shopping list of items you'll need (each day will differ on specific items though, so check through and make a list). Everything is available at well-stocked health food stores, magickal supply stores, new age and alternative product stores. Check out my website www.fionahorne.com for lists of international suppliers.

* *incense sticks*
* *candles*
* *herbs*
* *oils*
* *crystals*
* *charcoal discs*
* *tweezers or tongs (to hold the disc as you light it)*
* *matches*
* *sand*
* *heatproof bowl (put sand in the bottom and use to burn the charcoal disc on – a ceramic ashtray or clay dish is good)*
* *pestle and mortar for preparing incense*
* *Book of Shadows – a workbook in which to write up your experiences and insights (press a mulberry or bay leaf in it to guard its secrets – it's only for you to read!)*
* *aromatherapy oil burner*
* *Dream Diary – this can be a simple notebook in which you record your dreams. To analyze them, you can just use your intuition or buy a "dream dictionary." One I recommend is* **The Dictionary of Dreams** *by Gustavus Hindman Miller (Fireside)*

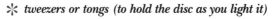

It may seem like there is a lot of stuff to get and to familiarize yourself with – but that's a good thing! I have suggested simple and easily attainable items alongside the more obscure ones if you are really stuck. But I urge you to track down the unusual herbs and other esoteric supplies to really get the most out of your makeover. Anything worthwhile takes effort and while elsewhere in this book there are lots of simple everyday things suggested to make your life more enchanting, the point of the seven-day magickal makeover is to transform you into a potent and powerful being. So roll up your sleeves and go for it – you're worth it!

GETTING STARTED

## YOUR MAGICKAL ALTAR

**It's a good idea to create an altar or shrine for the week. This serves to dedicate your space and support your bewitching efforts! Set it up somewhere visible so that every time you pass by you reaffirm your commitment to your magickal transformation. Also, if you like, throughout the day you can kneel for a moment to focus on your magickal tasks and repeat your morning affirmation. Your altar needs to feature the four elements – Fire, Earth, Water, and Air, and a few other things!**

✳ **FIRE:** *A thick white candle*
*(perhaps scented with vanilla for fresh energies)*

✳ **EARTH:** *A bowl of sea salt and/or a quartz crystal*

✳ **WATER:** *A chalice of spring water*
*(refill it every day and put a pinch of salt in for purity)*

✳ **AIR:** *Incense, an aromatherapy oil burner, or a feather*

✳ *Fresh flowers or a plant (to honor the Earth)*

✳ *An inspirational photo (perhaps of a Goddess image,*
*or of an animal whose qualities you admire, or of a beautiful*
*place that inspires in you a sense of peace)*

### KEEP A RECORD

You might like to get a Polaroid camera to take instant photos of your altar and ritual work – you will be making a record of your progress in your Book of Shadows to look back on and be inspired by later, so don't be afraid to get creative! For example, pressing some of the flowers from your different rituals and sealing them on the paper with drops of magickally charged wax from your candles will preserve the essence of your ritual work.

### ANOINTING OIL

Each day I have suggested an anointing oil to help
enhance your powers of transformation. Applying this
is not essential but will assist your magickal makeover.
Blend two or three drops of the suggested oils into a
teaspoon of a carrier oil, like almond, olive, wheat germ
or jojoba. Using the index finger of your dominant
hand, touch a little to your third eye – between your
eyebrows (home of your psychic self), your throat
(for communication), over your heart (for pure intent
and love), your solar plexus – just below the center
of your ribcage (for connectedness), and on top of
both your feet (so that you walk in grace).

Do this at sunrise and sunset with reverence – being
aware that you're not applying perfume but anointing
yourself with special oils blended for a magickal purpose.

### DAILY RITUALS

The following guidelines will form your structure
for each day; then you can carry out your daily magickal
work within these. There are affirmations to make,
special herbal teas to drink and specific tasks for you to
perform. The following provide a framework that can
be interspersed with other magickal activities of your
choice. (For example, analyzing your dream diary,
reading an inspiring book, watching a mystical movie
or making positive plans for the future – your only
guideline is that you should be selfish and only do
things that please and motivate you!)

### *On Waking*

Slowly stretch in your bed, luxuriating in your body.
Think about what an extraordinary being you are: a
human being capable of magnificent things, a Child of
the Universe. Just before you rise, think about how you
have set this week or day aside for yourself to explore and
cultivate your inner powers. Have your dream diary by
your bed and write down anything you remember and
consider significant so you can analyze your dreams. Take
note of any signs or insights that could influence your
practices for the coming day.

When you are ready, deeply inhale and exhale five times,
focusing on your breath as it moves slowly in and out
of your body. Rise, feeling peaceful and serene, rinse
your face, and head outside to your garden, balcony or
perhaps just an open window. With the sun and fresh air
on your face, perform the Pentagram Salute to the Sun.

### Pentagram Salute

With the right forefinger, touch your third eye (between
the eyebrows), left breast, right shoulder, left shoulder,
right breast and third eye again to complete the Witches'
sacred five-pointed star. As you do this, say either silently
or out aloud, "I dedicate myself in Perfect Love and
Perfect Trust to the Universal Forces of Magick."

### *Rinsing Your Face*

There is an ancient yogic way of rinsing your face in
the morning after sleep that puts you in a calm and
focused state. Hold some water in your mouth and splash
your face with your eyes open twelve times. Apparently
this stimulates a "diving response" and mimics the time
we were floating in the watery womb with our eyes
open and our lungs full of fluid. This practice triggers
deep in our memory the calm sense of oneness with
the world we felt at that time.

### *Be Pure*

#### PURIFYING ELIXIR

*You will need:*

⁕ *1.5 liters (½ gallon) of spring water*
⁕ *1 handful dried valerian (a valued Witches' herb
of purification – use lavender if you can't get this
as it is also an enchanted herb of purity)*
⁕ *1 piece of clear quartz crystal (to charge up the elixir)*

In a large saucepan, simmer the water and the herb five
minutes. Strain and put in a container with the crystal.
Shower with the intent not only to purify your body but
also to remove any excess energies you accumulated
whilst surfing the night planes (i.e. dreaming!).

After your shower, douse yourself from the neck down with a cup of the elixir. If you decided to take a bath, sponge yourself down with the elixir afterwards and lightly pat your body dry.

Now dress in the suggested attire for the day, and if you choose to wear make-up or go to a lot of trouble with your appearance at this point that's fine! Stir up those creative juices and exult in yourself! Personally, I love decorating myself by dusting MAC Cosmetics' glowing glitter pigment powders over my skin so that I shimmer like a Moon Goddess. Alternatively, be as bare as the day you popped out into the world.

✳ **TIP:** *Each day as a part of the evening ritual I suggest a magickal bath. If you don't have a bath, shower, then mix the described essential oils in a large container with warm water and sponge yourself, using a soft cloth.*

### *Chakra Meditation*

The following meditation should be done every morning and is not only to focus and center you for the day but to empower you by actively re-establishing the connection of your life force with that of the Universe.

*You will need:*

✳ *a long sarong or piece of material in a light color (pearly, pale blue would be good), long enough for you to lie stretched out on*
✳ *1 white candle*
✳ *1 red candle*

✳ **TIP:** *You might like to consider making a guide tape by recording yourself slowly reading through the meditation, so you don't have to try to remember anything and can just lose yourself in the visualizations.*

Lay out the sarong and light the candles, placing the red one at your feet and the white one at your head. Make sure they will each be at least a foot away from your body when you're lying stretched out.

Lie down on the sarong with the backs of your hands resting on the ground so that your palms are face up. (If you prefer you can do this meditation sitting up either on the sarong or in a chair – this is good for people who find it easy to drop off to sleep!) Relax your body. Take seven deep, slow breaths, feeling the air move not only through your lungs but through your whole body.

* *Concentrate on the first chakra at the base of your spine: the Root chakra. See it as a kind of "wheel" in an earthy deep red color – and feel it pulse. When that is clear, sense the wheel starting to spin in a deosil (sunwise/clockwise) direction. Feel the strong centering action of this first chakra as it spins. Now, see it extend as a beam of red light deep, deep down into the earth, grounding and connecting the core of your being with Gaia, the Earth Mother.*

* *When you sense your connection to be really strong, move your attention to the next chakra: the Base Sexual chakra, which is just above the pubic bone. See it as a clear, yet intense, orange, like a huge spark from a volcano, spinning and pulsing.*

* *Move to the next chakra, the Solar plexus, located at the base of the ribcage, the home of "gut" feelings. See it spin and pulse, its color pure yellow like marigolds.*

✳ *Next is the Heart chakra; see it spin and pulse a soft green, the color of delicate new blades of feathery grass.*

✳ *Move up to the Throat chakra, and see it spin and pulse the azure blue color of a fresh, clear daytime sky.*

✳ *Next is the Brow chakra, or "third eye," see it spin and pulse a rich, dark blue – the color of a deep tropical ocean.*

✳ *Finally, move your attention to the Crown chakra, a crystal-clear light purple, like a violet sky at sunrise. Concentrate on it spinning and pulsing, and as it does, feel the top of your head tingle as you open your Crown chakra to the Universe. See a bolt of infinite diamond white light come from the heavens and connect with your Crown.*

See the light charge through your glowing chakras, intensifying their colors and making them spin faster and faster. Then, see the white light shoot through the red cord of your Root chakra descending into the earth and feel how grounded you are as you are charged with the purest of energy. See your chakras glowing like a string of beautiful colored pearls and feel your whole being suffused with power.

When you are ready, slowly close your Crown and Root chakras. Do this by visualizing these chakras ceasing their spin and sealing off the energy, and then see the others gradually return to their original glowing state. Take three deep breaths and open your eyes. You will be charged and centered and ready for an amazing day!

## *Morning Affirmation*

Each day has a suggested morning affirmation. A good
time to say it is straight after your Chakra Meditation.
Either memorize the words or read them out aloud, slowly
and clearly. Do this three times and if you like you can
repeat the affirmation throughout the day to stay focused.

## *End of the Day Ritual*

After a hard day's magickal work, just before you go
to bed, stand out under the moon or face an open
window and again perform the Pentagram Salute. Take
a good Witchy novel to read in bed – I recommend
*Queen of the Witches* by Jessica Berens, Phyllis Curott's
autobiographical *Book of Shadows*, or maybe my book,
*Witch – A Magickal Journey*! Have your dream diary
next to the bed with a pen, ready for you to make notes
on your nighttime adventures first thing in the morning.

# monday

## PSYCHIC POWER UP!

**MONDAY is ruled by the Moon and is a day to connect with your deepest sense of self. On this day your powers of intuition and inspiration can be enhanced and developed so that you achieve a profound sense of personal peace and empowerment.**

**It is also a day for you to tap into your psychic powers and increase your skills of divination – looking into the future, or "between the worlds" for guidance and insight.**

**If you can line up your Monday on or near a full moon, so much the better.**

*Anointing Oil*

*One drop each of lavender, geranium and bergamot essential
oils in one teaspoon of a base oil (or just three drops of
geranium if there are budget constraints!).*

*Attire*

*Today wear white or perhaps pale lavender or silvery blue –
pure, simple, flowing, and uncluttered.*

## MONDAY AFFIRMATION

"I dedicate today to me
To increase my sensitivity
To unleash the powers within me
To know all that I can be."

Really focus on the meaning of the words and your desire
to be completely at one with yourself as you tap into your
hidden abilities.

### *Herbal Tea*

✳ **JASMINE:** *Night-blooming jasmine is sacred to the moon. Pick your own, and steep a handful of fresh petals to a pot. Or if you can't get hold of any fresh, buy Chinese jasmine tea. Have a cup with your meals if you like – it aids digestion.*

✳ **MUGWORT:** *Mugwort is a magickal tonic that heightens psychic awareness and inner vision. Three tablespoons of the dried leaf to a good size pot should be kept warm on the stove. Don't brew it too strongly, as you should drink at least four cups throughout the day. Sweeten with a little honey. Mugwort is available at most well stocked health food stores, but if you can't find any substitute with chamomile.*

## JUST ANOTHER MYSTIC MONDAY

Assemble your chosen tools of divination – Tarot cards,
a crystal ball, runes, tea leaves, whatever you are drawn
to. Treat the first part of the day as a time for study;
spend the morning reading and delving into your choice
of divinatory method to be prepared for the ritual later
in the evening. Today is a peaceful and reflective day,
so move slowly and if you can, allow your mind to
wander; be in a semi-meditational state all day. A cup of
mugwort tea, sweetened with honey and drunk every
three hours, will help you achieve this.

### DIVINE DREAM PILLOW

In the afternoon, make a Divine Dream Pillow. Placing
this under or next to your head as you sleep will bring
visions of the future and inner enlightenment.

*You will need:*

✳ *2 handfuls of dried mugwort (or chamomile)*
✳ *1 handful of lavender*
✳ *1 handful of black poppy seeds*
✳ *2 squares of purple velvet*
✳ *sandalwood incense sticks*

Create a sacred workspace by lighting one white candle
and burning sandalwood incense. Sew three edges of the
pillow together and stuff with the herbs and seeds.

Carefully sew closed. As you do this, chant this incantation:

"Dreams divine
Now be mine
In sleep serene
Secrets foreseen."

When you have made the pillow, pass it through the
smoke of the incense three times, as you say:

"Sacred moon smoke
I honor thee,
Your blessing evoked
One Two Three."

Have some more mugwort tea and then rest
for a while with your pillow under your head.
Have a notepad and pen near by.

As you close your eyes do the following meditation:

*You are nestled in a silver cloud —*
*soft and translucent — you are weightless as you float.*
*The glow of a full moon coats your skin in a heavenly*
*luster. You are perfect and serene.*
*Now feel the moonlight gently penetrate your skin*
*— taking your awareness within —*
*to the deepest core of yourself.*
*Be aware of how this feels,*
*trust that you are safe and allow any*
*feelings or thoughts to be revealed*
*nder the moon's pure penetrating light.*

When you are ready, open your eyes and write down
everything that was revealed – good and perhaps bad.
Put this aside for use later in your ritual. Now, if you like,
have a nap or take a gentle stroll in a park or beside the
ocean. Continue to let your mind wander and keep your
own counsel (that is, don't talk to anyone!)

## PREPARE FOR THE FUTURE — SUNSET RITUAL

As the sun sets it is time to prepare for your evening personal power ritual.

### *Incense*

*First blend some divination incense. Grind together two teaspoons of sandalwood, one teaspoon of orris root powder, four cloves, half a teaspoon of nutmeg and four drops of lemon oil.*

✳ **ALTERNATIVE:** *If you can't get any of the ingredients above, use jasmine stick incense.*

✳ **TIP:** *Making incense is very easy. First you need patience, then your ingredients and pestle and mortar. Always grind together dry ingredients first until they are powdery and well blended – then slowly add any essential oils drop by drop mixing through well.*

Select one or two particular Tarot cards or runes that you feel drawn to. If you are working with a crystal ball or tealeaves then choose an inspirational photograph that stirs your creative inspiration. Light a white candle and place the cards, runes, or picture in front. Burn your divination incense and meditate gazing at them. Think about what drew you to the images and what this says about you. When you are ready, make any relevant notes on insights gained or thoughts that crossed your mind in your Book of Shadows.

### PSYCHIC POWER RITUAL

This ritual should be done after your dinner –
try to eat lightly, as a very full stomach can make
it difficult to focus.

First set up a sacred space with three white and
three silver candles. Decorate the base of the candles
with white flowers to honor the Moon Goddess. Set
out a black or silver cloth upon which to do your
divinatory reading. Place amethyst, moonstone or black
obsidian crystal on your altar to enhance your
powers and have your divination tools ready. Light
the candles and burn more incense.

Now have a bath with six drops of your anointing oil blend added and drink another cup of mugwort tea to ready yourself for your ritual. Bathe by the light of one white candle and focus on your goal, which is to tap into your most profound sense of self and to use divination to reveal the way to releasing your personal power.

Do the ritual skyclad (naked – which is a pure and perfect state) or clothed in white, lavender, or pale blue.

You have created a sacred space in the physical realm, now it's time to create it in the astral realm. Call on the Triple Goddess to bless and witness your ritual:

*"Goddess of the Moon — Maiden/Mother/Crone*
*Illuminate my consciousness with your radiant glow."*

Meditate on your divinatory goals – determine these based on the insights you gained during your meditations today. Do you need more insight into a certain problem? Do you need clarification concerning your life's direction? Are you pretty happy with how you're developing and would enjoy some hints of the future? Do your reading from your chosen tool of divination as the divination incense burns, taking your time and giving full rein to your intuition. When you are ready, make a written record of all insights gained and the action you now know is necessary to deal with any problems.

When you have finished the reading, say this charm:

"Between the worlds
Come to me
Secrets of my being
All time is now
And I know how
To reveal the best in me."

Take time to relax and enjoy the beautiful ambience you have created. Feel a deep sense of connectedness and satisfaction. Know that any problems revealed today are now free and in the process of being solved. Know that you have tapped into your psychic powers and, with continued nurturing, they will grow and assist you.

When you are ready, snuff out the candles, do your End of Day Ritual, and sleep with your Divine Dream Pillow!

# tuesday

## SOLDIER ON

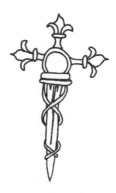

**TUESDAY is ruled by the planet Mars; it's a day to awaken your passion to excel and to develop the courage required for this. It's also a time to do rituals and activities to let go of anything in your life that just doesn't serve you anymore.**

### *Anointing Oil*

Three drops of pine oil in a carrier base.

### *Attire*

Wear red – the color of courage and valor.

## TUESDAY AFFIRMATION

"Today I am a warrior
Against stagnancy and fear
Today I am a warrior
So the way ahead is clear."

### *Herbal Tea*

✳ **GINSENG WITH GINGER ROOT ADDED:** *Ginseng is an excellent tonic. It encourages vitality and stimulates your psyche and physical body to feel capable and strong. Ginger is strengthening and in a magickal sense, protective. Drink at least five cups of this tea today. Buy the teabags and add a few slivers of fresh ginger root to a cup.*

## OUT WITH THE OLD

First have a really big clean up of your house and be brutal! This requires bravery, but purging the past frees the way to fresh perspectives, new energy, and strength of intent. Work with the prevailing energy of the Warrior Lord, Mars, by chanting this charm as you go:

"Fearless and proud
Bold and brave
Without hesitation
Decisions are made."

Vanquish everything that is trapping you in the past and holding you back: old letters, old photos, even clothing and furniture. Organize for the Salvation Army or another charity organization to come by and collect all the nicest items that you are letting go of for needy people to enjoy. Before you give them away, do a small purification ritual by holding a lit stick of frankincense incense as you circle the goods three times widdershins (counter-clockwise or against the direction of the sun), saying:

*"I banish any negativity stored here."*

Then circle the goods deosil (clockwise or with the sun) three times and say:

*"I imbue these goods with love and good will."*

When you have finished clearing out the dross, rearrange your furniture, or if that's not appropriate, rearrange any knick-knacks and tidy up your cupboards.

## GET SET TO LET GO

### *Incense*

*Now make a purification incense of one teaspoon of dragon's blood powder (use cayenne pepper if you can't get this), three pinches of tobacco, and half a teaspoon of frankincense resin (or two drops of frankincense or benzoin oil).*

✳ **ALTERNATIVE:** *If you can't get these, use a handful of frankincense incense sticks.*

At sunset open all the windows and doors to put a breath of fresh air into your surroundings and release any trapped energy, and perform the following ritual.

In a heatproof bowl, light two charcoal discs and sprinkle them with your purification incense. Walk from room to room, fanning the smoke outward with your hand, saying:

*"I release and put weakness to rest*
*With pride and strength I hold my head*
*High as the sun sets on the past*
*New beginnings, new passion, courage that lasts."*

When you have completely fumigated your space and the sun has set, close all the doors and windows – anything you opened. Now that you have dealt with your surroundings, it's time for an inner cleansing.

✳ **TIP:** *Try to memorize your incantations and affirmations so that you can really concentrate. Magick will only enter your life if you focus and believe that it can.*

## THE RITUAL OF RELEASE

Decorate your space with eight orange and white
candles, and red flowers. If you have a large cast-iron
pot (or even a cauldron!), place some sand in the bottom
and stand it in the center of the space on a heatproof
mat. If you don't have a pot, have a black candle ready
and a heatproof container beside it. Also have ready a
piece of red paper and a black pen.

### *Incense*

***Blend incense made of two teaspoons of sandalwood powder
with three drops of frankincense oil.***

✳ **ALTERNATIVE:** *Use sticks of sandalwood
and frankincense incense.*

For this ritual you need to wear an amulet of ginger root for protection and fortitude. Make this by tying a piece of red cord around the root, leaving the cord long enough to fasten around your neck.

By the light of a red candle, have a bath to which you have added four drops of pine oil. Whilst you are bathing, meditate on what you have achieved today and how you are freeing up your world so that you can function more courageously and effectively in all ways.

Do this ritual either skyclad or clothed in red. Place your amulet around your neck. Now carry the candle to your workspace and use it to light the other candles and incense. Sit and close your eyes, deeply inhale the scented air, and call on the Avenging Warlord, Mars.

"Mars! I call upon your presence
Fill me with your strength
Reveal my inner enemy
Destroy that which oppresses me."

Feel Mars' power roar through your veins. Recognize the things in your psyche that are blocking you – old fears, old desires – and write them down on the paper, as Mars' mighty sword slashes the bonds that bind them to you. When you have purged everything, crush the paper into a ball and throw it into the cauldron to set fire to it (or burn it in the flame of the black candle, letting the ashes settle in the heatproof bowl).

When the final embers have died clap three times and say:

*"It is done."*

Rest for a moment and enjoy the sense of clarity and peace you feel now. Conflict is gone. Meditate on the qualities of courage, endurance, and virtue. When you are ready, bury the ashes in earth (either outside or in a planter box) with your ginger root amulet and do your End of Day Ritual. Sleep well!

# wednesday

WISE UP!

**WEDNESDAY is ruled by the planet Mercury and is therefore a day to store up on knowledge and develop your powers of wisdom (which is different to knowledge!). In today's society the acquisition of facts is seen as all-important, but this is not the same as understanding. Wisdom comes when you not only exercise your rational mind, but flex your creative and imaginative muscles too.**

### *Anointing Oil*

One drop each of lemon, rosemary and mandarin oil
in a carrier base (or just three drops of mandarin).

### *Attire*

Wear purple – the color of wisdom and insight.

## WEDNESDAY AFFIRMATION

"Information knowing and wisdom flowing
Powers of perception growing and growing
My imagination is the right key
For unlocking true wisdom inside me."

### *Herbal Tea*

✳ **ROSEMARY:** *Rosemary is traditionally known as the herb of remembrance – it stimulates the memory. Make a brew using a teaspoon of the dried herb to a cup and drink with your meals.*

✳ **SAGE:** *Sage is a brain nourisher – it works to sweep away the cobwebs and encourage clear and perceptive thinking. Drink at least three cups of this today.*

✳ **TIP:** *The herbs I've suggested for the teas can be drunk alone, or you may like to find a blend that features the suggested herb in your health food store.*

## YEARN TO LEARN

First make a list of things that you would like to expand
your knowledge on. Are you drawn to Witchcraft and
wanting to explore it further? Or are you a student and

having trouble studying and remembering information
at exam time? Or do you have to present reports at
work and sometimes a grasp of all the data eludes you?
Or do you want to learn a musical instrument but are
scared that it will take too long to learn? Or on the other
hand, is your quest not so much about retaining facts and
figures but more about personal issues? For example, do
you keep repeating the same situations in your life (like
destructive relationships) without learning and moving on?

Today you will open up the doors of your mind and free
your powers of pursuing and retaining knowledge. At
the same time, you will tap into and develop your powers
of wisdom, by using your imagination.

Spend the morning relaxing and reading on subjects
that interest you. Have a pad and pen, and make notes
on how you absorb and process information. Do you
read fast and skim over topics so that you only get a basic
grasp? Do you read really thoroughly and obsess over
remembering dates and names? Do you feel intimidated
because it's all too hard and you'll never remember all
this? Or can you absorb all the facts in the world, but you
still feel uninspired?

## DO THE WRITE THING!

In the afternoon, it's time to exercise your imagination.
Have a good look at the notes that you've made –
what do they say about you? Are you impatient? Fearful?
Nervous? Have a cup of sage tea and a good think
about how you would like to transform yourself.

When you are ready write a myth – a creative story
about your situation and how you would like to change it.
You don't have to be the standard of a professional
writer – the point of this exercise is to create a new
vision of yourself.

Don't limit yourself, take your time and find an alternative way of describing your current situation. For example, you tend to read fast and get impatient, you are bored easily and don't feel really passionate about what you have to study for your exams, so you write the following story:

*A princess lives in a tower, her mother, the Queen has locked her there and will only let her go when she can recite all the names of all the queens that ever lived. There are reasons for this — one day the princess will be queen and must know of her ancestors if she is to govern well. But all the princess wants to do is play with her friends and ride her horses. She tries and tries but can not remember — her head is full of other people and other places.*

*One day a bird lands on her windowsill and says to her, "For a whole year I have flown by this window and you are always sitting here looking sad."*

*The princess says to the bird, "My mother has locked me here until I learn of all the queens that ever lived, but I just can't — I want to play outside with the other princesses."*

*The bird says, "Then it's obvious, your only choice is to put the others out of your head and make the queens your friends. Play with them here instead. Then you won't feel lonely and left out, but have all new friends to play with — in your mind!"*

*The princess looked at the bird in astonishment. Of course, it all made sense, she would make friends with all the queens! She thanked the bird and went back to her books, learning all the names and interesting stories of her new friends. She traveled to faraway places on the back of the warrior Queen Nirvana's white horse and enjoyed fine dinners with Queen Laeticia at her castle in Spain.*

*When the princess's mother came to ask her if she knew the queens, the princess had wonderful stories to tell of her new friends and the Queen released her. But something had changed in the princess: she realized that her place within the world of knowledge and imagination was more exciting than she ever thought possible. And she grew up to be the wisest Queen there ever was.*

When you are finished, copy the myth into your Book of Shadows. You may like to illustrate your myth by drawing or decorating with pictures cut from magazines – be as creative as you like. The more inspiring images you weave together the more effective the transformation.

### READY, STEADY, KNOW!

#### *Incense*

*Blend incense made of one teaspoon of mace, one teaspoon of ground cedar and half a teaspoon of nutmeg.*

✳ **ALTERNATIVE:** *If you can't get these ingredients, burn lavender or rosemary stick incense.*

In the evening, set up a space with six purple candles and bunches of lavender and other purple flowers (irises are a good choice as they have been associated with wisdom since the time of the ancient Egyptians). You will also need a bowl of spring water and a piece of bloodstone (a charmed crystal for the getting of wisdom).

Place your Book of Shadows, opened to your myth,
in the center of your ritual space.

Have a bath to which you have added six drops of your
anointing oil. Bathe by the light of a purple candle and
meditate upon how acquiring knowledge is not so hard –
it's having the wisdom to use it well that is the challenge.

### RITUAL FOR WISDOM AND KNOWLEDGE

Be skyclad or clothed in purple as you sit in your space.
Gaze at the candle flames and focus on your desire to be
knowledgeable and wise, and invoke the Greek Goddess
of Wisdom, Athena, and the Greek God of Intelligence,
Hermes, by saying this invocation:

"Wise and benevolent, Athena and Hermes,
Witness and bless this rite of knowledge.
Assist me in unlocking my potential
Knowledge and wisdom are now essential
For me to achieve all my goals
In all areas of life as they unfold."

Now consecrate and bless your myth with the four elements. Fan incense smoke over it for Air and say:

"Blessed are my efforts by Air."

Sprinkle the book with salt for Earth and say:

"Blessed are my efforts by Earth."

Sprinkle around it with a little Water and say:

*"Blessed are my efforts by Water."*

Then hold it up to the light of the candles and say:

*"Blessed are my efforts by Fire."*

Hold the bloodstone in your hand, read your myth out aloud, and again focus on its meaning and message. Spend some time meditating on how you have transformed your perception of yourself and your abilities. In your mind's eye, see yourself dealing with situations in new and wiser ways.

If you like, make a note in your Book of Shadows of any further insights you gain. When you are finished, snuff the candles and do your End of Day Ritual.

# thursday

# SHOW ME THE MONEY!

**THURSDAY** is ruled by Jupiter who represents good luck, generosity, wealth (not just financially but of spirit), and favorable legal outcomes! So today is the time to do rituals for good fortune and prosperity and cultivate in yourself the knowledge that you deserve the very best in all things.

### *Anointing Oil*

One drop of frankincense, sandalwood and myrrh in
carrier oil (or just three drops of bergamot oil).

### *Attire*

Today, wear green clothing for prosperity, luck,
and good fortune.

### THURSDAY AFFIRMATION

"Today grants me good fortune
In every way I choose
As I focus all my efforts
I really cannot lose."

### *Herbal Tea*

✳ **BERRY TEAS:** *Raspberry, blackberry, blueberry. Berries represent opulence and good fortune – drinking their tea invigorates the senses.*

✳ **BERGAMOT:** *In other words, Earl Grey tea! The unique scent and flavor is conferred by the rind of the Italian fruit bergamot (a miniature pear-shaped orange), which is a prosperity drawing charm.*

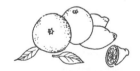

Decide what it is you want to focus on. Increasing your financial wealth goes hand in hand with increasing your confidence so that you feel worthy of riches. A favorable outcome in a legal battle or a wage rise that you feel you deserve goes hand in hand with honesty and effort. You can either do all the following rituals or focus on the ones that specifically deal with your concerns. When you are not doing the rituals, relax and read an inspiring biography about someone who has overcome adversity to flourish and prosper. Also make notes and plans for ways that increased prosperity and good fortune can manifest in your life for use during the evening ritual.

✳ **TIP:** *If you like, throughout the day you can play music that inspires but does not distract you.*

## MORNING:
## RITUAL FOR CAREER ADVANCES
## AND FOR DECISIONS
## TO BE MADE IN YOUR FAVOR

For this ritual you will need a seedling plant of either
mint (for the ability to flourish) or bay laurel (for
good luck and protection). If you are hoping a decision
will go your way, plant motherwort (for confidence
and reassurance that the best outcome will result).
If your goal is a little of all of the above – plant sage.
You will also need a larger pot and potting mix.
Light an orange candle, which has been anointed
with two drops of bergamot oil, standing it in a
heatproof bowl.

On one white piece of paper, write a detailed description
of your current situation that you are concerned about.
For example:

"I feel stuck in my boring job. I want a promotion to a
more exciting position," or "I am concerned that the
court case is not going to go my way."

Study what you have written for a moment; if any
additional comments come to mind, jot them down.

Now on a green piece of paper, write a detailed
description of your desired outcome – be as specific as
you can. Study this for a moment and try to actually see
yourself once the favorable outcome has resulted; notice
your emotions, your sense of elation and satisfaction.

When these images and feelings are strong,
kiss the paper three times and say, "So Be It."

Now fold the paper into a small square and place it in the larger pot. Fill the pot with potting mix and plant the seedling. As you do this, say this charm:

"Sacred herb of holy power
Bless my wish, make it flower
Help fulfill my dreams and goals
So my destiny I control."

Blow your breath over the plant three times to infuse it with your life energy and forge a strong bond.

Now burn the white paper and turn the ashes into the new soil as you say:

"The past I now release
To nurture a future of ease."

Place the plant by your altar space for the rest of the day and continue to nurture it – as the plant grows, so will your desired outcome.

## AFTERNOON:
## RITUAL TO BRING MONEY

### *Incense*

*Make incense by blending one teaspoon of High John the Conqueror powder (otherwise known as the spice galangal), one teaspoon of sandalwood and two drops of patchouli oil.*

✳ **ALTERNATIVE:** *Burn one stick of sandalwood and one stick of patchouli incense.*

Set up a workspace with two gold and two green candles placed around a heatproof bowl, 'play money' (Monopoly money or similar), a small bowl of earth or sand, and a goblet or bowl of water. You will also need a piece of peridot crystal (helps to release fear and encourages money to flow).

Burn the incense and sip some Earl Grey tea as you gaze
at the candle flames and think about your relationship
with money. Do you feel deep down you will never really
have as much as you desire and never really apply
yourself to make more?

Do you wish you'd win the lottery? Do you spend it faster
than you earn it? Are you greedy and expect more than
you need – so nothing comes at all? Make some notes on
a piece of paper and be honest.

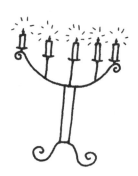

Now hold the crystal in your hand and calmly say
this incantation three times:

"My rightful state is prosperity
I release my fears of poverty."

You are now going to burn the money, but this is not to
say that you are destroying it – rather, you are freeing
up your previous ways of relating to money and allowing
for a new relationship with it. You will also burn the notes
you made about your previous financial attitude
and situation, to release them and allow for new,
more prosperous behavior to develop.

So light the money with the flames of the candles
and toss it into the heatproof bowl. As it burns, throw in
your notes and say forcefully:

"I free myself of what was previously
Money is now coming to me
I give up the way I was before
Money manifests by the power of four
One for fire as money burns
Two for air as incense churns"

(fan the incense over the burning money)

"Three for water to quench fear"

(sprinkle a little water on burning money)

"Four for earth — success is near"

(cover the ashes with earth)

Now take the ashes and earth outside and sprinkle them over the ground.

Spend the rest of the afternoon writing up a plan of the action that you will take on the physical plane now that you have freed up the astral plane. Will you apply for a new job, take a course so that you are qualified for a better position, hold a garage sale, or apply for a grant? Get excited and passionate, knowing that any plans you put into action now will manifest as you desire. Write up everything in your Book of Shadows.

### EVENING:
### RITUAL FOR GOOD LUCK
### AND GOOD FORTUNE

You are going to make a charm bag that is magickally charged and will act as a magnet to draw luck and good fortune to you.

*You will need:*

✳ *1 green velvet pouch*
✳ *frankincense*
*(for opulence and blessed by Jupiter)*
✳ *3 saffron threads (for luck and good fortune)*
✳ *1 piece of tin – 1 inch/2 cm square*
*(to attract and money and goods and governed by Jupiter)*
✳ *1 peridot crystal from the previous ritual*
✳ *3 shavings of gold wax from a candle*
*used in your previous ritual*
✳ *1 lock of your hair*
✳ *1 sharp nail*
✳ *sandalwood incense for consecration of the bag*

Take a bath into which you have added a teaspoon of mustard seeds. This will rev up your circulation and help to charge up your intent. Bathe by the light of a gold candle and dress in green or gold for this ritual.

Using the following method, work out your personal magickal number.

Write out your date of birth in numerals. For example: July 7, 1975 would be 7.7.1975. Now add these together: 7 + 7 + 1 + 9 + 7 + 5 = 36. Reduce these to a single number: 3 + 6 = 9. So your number is nine. Reduce your numbers down to one digit unless they are 11 or 22, in which case leave them as double digits.

Carve this number into the tin using the sharp nail, then lick your thumb and trace over the carving. The tin is now charged with your essence and will work just for you.

Place all the ingredients into the bag, blow three
breaths into it, and draw the string closed tight.
Pass through the sandalwood smoke as you say:

*"Charm bag you are now potent
And working for me and my intent
Draw to me good luck and fortune
So to the best I am attuned."*

Keep the bag with you every day for seven days, after
which you can leave it where you sleep. Continue to
charge it up by passing through the sacred smoke of
sandalwood every Thursday and repeating the above charm.

Now perform your End of Day Ritual and get to bed –
you must be exhausted from all that spellcasting!

friday

ALL YOU NEED
IS LOVE

**FRIDAY** is ruled by Venus and so is a day to devote to self-love and love for all humanity. Today you will pamper yourself and nurture a sense of unconditional self-acceptance and appreciation; the benefits of this will flow into all areas of your life.

### *Anointing Oil*

One drop each of rose geranium, orange and ylang ylang
in a carrier base (or just three drops of ylang ylang).

### *Attire*

Dress in pinks and reds or, alternatively,
your absolutely favorite color.

✳ TIP: *I have suggested certain colored clothing, aligned to
your daily magickal goals. If you can't wear the complete
color, wear at least one item that corresponds to the power
color suggested. Except where I have suggested simplicity, dress
opulently and creatively – as well as feeling magickal, you
want to look magickal!*

### FRIDAY AFFIRMATION

"Sensual pleasure and spiritual light
Bless me today as is my right
Beauty and joy to have and hold
As a day of love unfolds."

### Herbal Tea

✳ **WILD STRAWBERRY:** *For happiness and love,*
*sweeten further with honey.*

✳ **ROSE:** *The ultimate flower of love! Steep three handfuls of*
*richly scented, fresh petals in almost boiling water and strain.*

First, book yourself in for a facial at your favorite
local beauty salon and/or organize for a mobile masseuse
to come around and massage your cares away! Burn
ylang ylang oil in an oil burner to fill your home with a
sensual, seductive scent. Lie around and eat delicious
foods – fresh succulent fruits and sweet chocolate.
Read beautiful poetry and inspiring verse to enrich your
heart. You may also like to read a book on human
biology, to more fully comprehend how your ultimate
and most valuable possession – your body – is one of
the most miraculous creations in all the Universe.

## YOUR PERSONAL SHRINE

Your main transformational task today is to make a
personal shrine just for you. Gather photos of yourself
of when you were a baby right through to the present
and arrange them attractively, wreathed by sunny
marigolds and heartsease (pansies) – or your favorite
flowers. Arrange amongst them pale pink and green
candles. On small pieces of pink paper, and using a silver
pen, write down lovely things you have done for yourself
and others throughout your life. Add anything further
to your shrine that you like – maybe a trophy or an
award, anything that makes you feel proud.

When your shrine is complete, meditate on your photos.
Look at a baby photo and gaze into your young eyes.
Think about all the things you've seen and done since
that photo was taken. Take the time to acknowledge how
you have grown and all your phenomenal achievements,
which are often what we take most for granted – learning
to walk, learning to speak, learning to love and desire
and live. Become very aware of how, despite the
difficulties of life, you are one of Life's biggest success
stories! You are a Child of the Universe.

Now, on a piece of pink paper, write a letter to yourself
as if you were a person who had just fallen in love with
you. Don't be shy, let your adoration pour out onto the
paper – you might feel a bit silly at first, but persevere!

When it is written, roll it up and place it on
your shrine. Light a stick of sandalwood incense,
and fan the smoke over the shrine as you say:

"I dedicate this shrine to me
To celebrate my purity
I dedicate this shrine to me
To celebrate my honesty
I dedicate this shrine to me
To celebrate my beauty."

Leave the stick of sandalwood burning to continue
honoring your life and take a photo to put in your Book
of Shadows (when you pack away your shrine be sure
to also paste the letter and all your reveries into
your Book of Shadows).

## CHARMED MOISTURIZER

Later in the day you might like to make some
"Charmed Moisturizer."

*You will need:*

✳ *1 handful of scented rose petals*
✳ *1 handful of marigold petals*
✳ *1 teaspoon of orris root powder (optional)*
✳ *1 tablespoon of rose water*
✳ *1 pint (568 ml) boiling water*
✳ *4 oz (115 g) of neutral, unscented moisturizing cream*
✳ *a sterilized glass container (boil in water)*

Steep the petals in the boiling water for 10 minutes to make a potent infusion and then strain. Put the moisturizer into a glass or china bowl and whisk in the infusion and rose water. Keep mixing until the cream cools and thickens (if it's too runny add the orris root powder). As you stir repeat this charm:

"Flowers of beauty
Bestow on me
Loveliness
For all to see."

Put your Charmed Moisturizer into the sterilized glass container and keep it in the fridge. Use it all over your body to enhance your natural beauty.

## RITUAL OF LOVE AND BEAUTY

*Incense*

*Make unconditional love incense by grinding together
two teaspoons of vervain, one teaspoon of dragon's blood
powder, one handful of dried rose petals, three drops
of lavender and two of clary sage oil.*

✳ **ALTERNATIVE:** *Burn sticks of rose incense.*

At sunset, set your workspace with three pink candles
and three light green candles, pink roses or other lush
pink flowers, and a mirror (either small or full length).
Have a bath into which you have placed six drops of your
anointing oil or six drops of ylang ylang. Bathe by the
light of a pink candle and play beautiful, relaxing music.
Do this ritual skyclad (a sacred state and perfect for this
particular ritual) or clothed in your favorite garment.
Call on the Greek Goddess of Love:

"*Sweet Goddess of Love, Aphrodite,*
*Enlighten me with your being*
*Witness and bless my rite*
*Of self-love and healing.*"

Take some time to gaze at your reflection in the mirror and feel unconditional self-love. Think about everything you have experienced today and what a beautiful day it has been. If you have trouble looking at yourself in the mirror, ask for help from Aphrodite again, and know that you have every right to feel love and appreciation for yourself within the sacred and safe place that you have created. If you have hang-ups about your physical shape, do this ritual skyclad and be accepting and proud of your wonderful and unique body.

When you are ready, keep looking at yourself and say:

"(Your name), you are blessed
By the Moon, the Sun and the Stars,
You are a Child of the Universe,
Perfect just the way you are."

Raise your personal power by passionately focusing
on the feelings of love that you have for your loved
ones and favorite things. (If you feel comfortable,
raise your personal power by masturbating to orgasm.)
When you feel sufficiently full of love, send the blissful,
ecstatic energy outwards to all people on the planet,
acknowledging that we are all one, and say:

"The power of love
Blesses and unites
All creation in holy light."

Snuff out your candles, do your End of Day Ritual
and enjoy beautiful dreams!

# saturday

## FORGIVE AND FORGET

**SATURDAY** is ruled by the planet Saturn and is a day
where you can be empowered to release fear, pain,
resentment, and negativity. Today you can literally
exorcise any very strong feelings of anger and hatred,
and heal yourself by tapping into your darkest feelings
and unleashing them as a purging experience.

### *Anointing oil*

Two drops of camphor in a carrier oil.

### *Attire*

Black for the ritual, white for after the ritual.

## SATURDAY AFFIRMATION

*"Today I cast out all my woes
Resentment and pain are free to go
No malice or punishment shall be given
All who wronged me now forgiven."*

### *Herbal Tea*

❋ **ANGELICA:** *A pleasant tasting tea that protects and heals.*

❋ **YARROW:** *The Irish think this to be the first herb baby Jesus picked, and it is considered a great charm against evil and sadness. It also works to heal a broken heart.*

❋ **LEMON AND GARLIC:** *If you have a lot of negative dross to free up, you can drink hot water with lemon, in which a clove of garlic has been soaked for a few minutes – garlic is renowned for its ability to exorcise evil (think of vampires!).*

❋ **DILL:** *This tea is for consumption after the ritual, as it is calming. Steep a small handful of the stem and leaves in a cup of boiling water, covered for 5 minutes – strain and sip.*

### GOODBYE BAD GUY

Today is the day that you get mad and allow yourself
to feel the power of your rage. The main ritual of today
needs to be done at sunset, so for the earlier part of the
day think about what makes or has made you incredibly
angry, harbor enormous resentment and probably
sadness (anger and sadness are often the same thing).
Throughout the day, allow it to build inside of you.
Listen to music that fires up your fury and think about
those who have hurt you and betrayed your trust,
whether physically, mentally, or spiritually: ex-boyfriends,
ex-school mates, even criminals like rapists whose crimes
have horrified you. Write, on black paper in red pen,
the ills and wrongs whose residue you wish to remove
from your consciousness for good.

To further facilitate your rage before your ritual you can drink some wine to which the powdered root of angelica has been added (¹/₄ teaspoon to one glass). This will work to release your inhibitions but at the same time protect you. Don't have more than two glasses – that is don't drink yourself into oblivion – you want your blood so hot that it burns your veins, but you want to be in control and able to gauge your limits before you transcend them. If you do not wish to drink alcohol then continue to consume the teas suggested above.

Today's work is likely to confront you with old feelings of
sadness you may not want to drag up. But these powers of
anger, resentment, and hatred are as valid as the powers
of love and compassion. They should be respected and
acknowledged, and it is empowering be able to tap into
them on call and with control. So this experience is not
only very cathartic, but also a vehicle for self-growth.

## IN THE EYE OF THE STORM

### *Incense*

*For your ritual make incense to honor the Hindu Goddess
of Destruction and Creation, Kali. Her action is swift –
she destroys what is wrong and then gives birth to what
is right. Grind together four teaspoons of mandrake
(or if you don't have it, comfrey), one teaspoon of henbane
(if you have it; use horehound if you don't),
one teaspoon of myrrh and eight drops of patchouli oil.*

✳ **ALTERNATIVE:** *Burn patchouli and myrrh stick incense.*

At sunset, prepare for the ritual. Do it in the bathroom, as you need somewhere you can get messy and then get clean. Prepare your space with eight black candles anointed with camphor oil. Have one white candle, anointed with neroli oil, put aside (if you don't have neroli, spray with a little of your favorite perfume). You will need either black water-based paint or, if your skin may react, a tube of cosmetic mud mask, black or dark green in color. You also need some beautiful soap – I recommend a natural soap, particularly with almond, sandalwood, or lavender oils and some lovely rich moisturizing lotion (your Charmed Moisturizer if you made some on Friday). And a lovely, fluffy white towel.

✳ **TIP:** *Anointing candles means to rub a drop or two of the suggested oil into the wax to charge and imbue the candle with magickal intent.*

## RITUAL OF RAGE AND RENEWAL

Begin the ritual by removing your clothes, then close
your eyes and invoke the ancient Goddess Kali:

*"Kali, Goddess of Retribution,
I call your powers of destruction
Illuminate what is concealed
Help me release the pain I feel."*

Read the list that you created during the day. Meditate
on the things that have caused you sadness and fury
and, as you do so acknowledge your inner pain by
marking yourself with the black paint or mud. If you
have physical scars from any cruelty inflicted on you,
swipe them with black paint as well. Bring all of the
pain that is inside up to the surface, and cry and scream;
lose yourself in your pain, in your fear, your anger.
Paint the names of people who have wronged you on
your skin – bring it all up to the surface.

When you are ready, acknowledge yourself
in the mirror and again call on Kali:

"Kali, Goddess of Retribution,
Bless me with your creation,
Now I may be cleansed and free
Of all that once did trouble me."

Tear up your notes forcefully and throw them in the bin.
Turn on the shower so that the water is fast and hot.
Stand under it and watch the blackness drain away. As it
goes down the drain, you will probably feel like crying
again but they will be tears of release. Let them wash
away in the cleansing water too. Soap yourself in a rich,
creamy lather, rinsing all traces of negativity away.

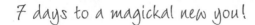 

When you are ready, get out of the shower and snuff the black candles. Light the white candle and gently towel yourself dry. Massage the moisturizing lotion gently into your body, feeling free and cleansed and healed.

Now make some dill tea and just relax for the rest of the evening, watch a beautiful movie, read a wonderful book, do your End of Day Ritual, and sleep like a baby!

*sunday*

IT'S A
BEAUTIFUL
WORLD

**SUNDAY** is ruled by our closest star, the Sun.

Today take advantage of its "wealth of spirit"

aspect to commune with the elements and nature.

In other words, you're going on a picnic!

### *Anointing Oil*

One drop of orange, clary sage, and ylang ylang in a
carrier base or just three drops of clary sage.

### *Attire*

Blue for harmony or orange for the sun – or both!
Wear clothing that is easy to tramp around the
countryside in, but make sure you look festive
and gorgeous!

### SUNDAY AFFIRMATION

"Today I celebrate my life
And share goodwill with all alive
I honor nature and my place
In a beautiful world full of grace."

### *Herbal tea*

✳ **TANSY:** *Considered a herb of immortality, it will help you comprehend the eternal nature of the life force.*

✳ **CHAMOMILE:** *Steeped with orange rind and a pinch each of cinnamon, nutmeg, and clove – perfect to honor the life-giving powers of the sun.*

Wake up to watch the sun rise and do some kind of yoga or stretching activity in the morning sun. Feel its rays penetrate your skin, warming and brightening your place in the Universe. (If it's cloudy be aware of all the sunlight beaming just above those clouds!) Eat a light breakfast and start to prepare for your magickal picnic.

## THE PERFECT PICNIC

The foods are simple and fresh yet all the ingredients have magickal significance. So don't smother the pasta in cheese or add ice cream to the apples! As you eat this food today you are taking part in a sacred ritual, and it is important that you focus and consume the foods with magickal intent.

✳ *Make fresh semolina pasta dressed with olives
(to honor the Sun God), parsley (to honor the Goddess),
thyme (to help commune with nature spirits),
"love apples" – tomatoes! (for blessings), and walnuts
(governed by the sun). Toss in virgin olive oil in which
a crushed bulb of garlic, eight sprigs of thyme,
eight juniper berries (for good health and energy)
and a teaspoon of black peppercorns (for enthusiasm)
have been steeped since yesterday.*

✳ *Home-baked corn bread (to celebrate the fertility
and sustenance of the land).*

✳ *Apples (for love) chopped and tossed in honey and little black currants (for sweet feelings and happiness).*

✳ *Wine (to honor the fruitfulness of the land) –*
*if you like, enjoy a sweet fruity wine, otherwise sweet*
*grape juice or sparkling mineral water is perfect. Dip a bay*
*leaf in each glass before you drink it, as a blessing.*

Use either a dark blue or green picnic blanket
or cloth, and take a beautiful goblet or glass to drink
from. Pack your picnic basket with the food and
drink, plates and cutlery. You will also need four dark
blue candles for your ritual (try to buy the candles that
are in a glass vase, so that outside breezes don't blow
them out), incense, and a heatproof bowl and charcoal
discs to burn in it. Don't take a book to read, just
take your Book of Shadows to record any inspiring
thoughts or insights that you have today.

Choose a beautiful place and one where you can easily
enjoy not only Air and Earth, but Fire and Water. Perhaps
a secluded beach, a lovely old park with a pond –
somewhere you can get to reasonably easily and not so
remote that you won't feel safe. If you have a lovely garden
with a pond or something similar, you may choose to stay
at home. Don't call off the day if it's raining – if it's private,
you can stand skyclad in the rain to connect with Water.

### *Incense*

*Prepare some "communing with nature" incense by mixing together three teaspoons of sandalwood, three teaspoons of dried lavender, one teaspoon of violet petals (or another scented blossom like jasmine, gardenia, or rose), and five drops of rose geranium oil. As you are blending your own incense repeat this charm:*

"Love and good tidings shall abound
When holy smoke scents all around."

✳ **ALTERNATIVE:** *Burn sticks of geranium or gardenia incense.*

## AT ONE WITH ALL THINGS

When you arrive, set up your space on a flat surface with
the candles at the four quarters of your blanket. Provided
the place you've chosen is sufficiently secluded but safe,
(and it's not too cold!) you may choose to work skyclad
to increase your contact with the world around you.

Lay out your foods and then sit in the center of
your blanket with your hands raised to the sky. Invoke
the God of Nature, Pan, and the great Earth Mother,
Gaia, with these words:

*"Great nurturing Mother Gaia and lusty*
*Lord of the Forests, Pan, I give thanks surrounded*
*by your beauty and the abundance of the land.*
*Cradled in your embrace I am blessed and I am aware*
*That everything begins and ends under your loving care."*

Enjoy your feast, crumbling some food and pouring
some drink on the ground as an offering to the
Gods. Soak up the natural environment and, as you
eat, be aware that you are born of the same elements
of everything that surrounds you. Feel your deep
and innate connection to the extraordinary biosphere
that is your home, Planet Earth.

When you have finished eating, it is time to align
yourself with the elements. Lie flat on the ground
and absorb the ancient energy of Earth. See in your
mind's eye the reality that you are lying on a huge
planet, spinning in space. When your body is
resonating with Earth's vibrations say:

*"I am born of Earth, I am blessed by Earth."*

Now stand up, close your eyes and sense the air
around you. Be aware of any subtle breezes or strong
gusts of wind. When you are ready say:

*"I am born of Air, I am blessed by Air."*

Now sit in front of the fire (or hold a candle in both hands). Feel the warmth of the flames (cup your hand around the candle flame if necessary) and watch their movement. Allow yourself to be mesmerized. Think of the molten flames at the core of the planet you stand on and the fiery form of the sun that is above you.
When you are ready say:

"I am born of Fire, I am blessed by Fire."

Now go for a swim in the ocean, or dip your feet in a pond, or stand out in the rain – commune with Water in the way you have chosen. Think of oceans of the planet; think of your body, composed of 70 percent water, feel yourself immersed in its flowing and healing qualities.
When you are ready say:

"I am born of Water, I am blessed by Water."

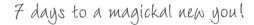
Meditate again on how you are evolved of this planet,
how its life is your life. After your meditation, relax
and keep enjoying the great outdoors!

When you are ready to leave, make sure that you take
everything with you and leave not a trace of your
presence (except perhaps an offering of a lock of your
hair, anchored in place with a stone or tied to a twig).

When you get home, get on the Internet or make some phone calls (you may have to do this one Monday morning) to take the necessary steps to join an environmental conservation group (if you're not already a member). If you visit my website, www.fionahorne.com go to "Gaia Gateway" where you will find lots of links and information. Hire some videos of nature and animal documentaries and spend the evening enjoying more of the immense wonders of our beautiful planet.

Finish with your End of Day Ritual and dream of travelling to visit these places one day soon!

# mini makeover

## EVERYDAY MAGICK

Okay, you just can't see yourself getting one day free
over the next two months – let alone a week! But you
want to inject a bit more magick into your life NOW –
what can you do? Well, lots of things! When you are first
drawn to magick and Witchcraft, you can think,
"I have to completely overhaul my life, I don't know
where to start, it's all too hard." So you read a nice book
and then put it down and don't do anything about it.
Well, the best way to uncover your hidden powers is to
start doing little things every day.

You can perform the Pentagram Salute to the Sun
every morning and night any day. It's a great way
to align yourself to universal magickal forces and
reaffirm your interest and commitment to exploring
your hidden powers.

Take the time to make your living and working
environment magickal – burn incense instead of spraying
air fresheners, or burn aromatherapy oils. Fill your
house and office with living plants and flowers and
beautiful things. Buy yourself a certain colored flower
aligned to a magickal purpose on the way to work,
pin it on your top or keep it in a vase and it will help
you focus your efforts and achieve your goals.

### *Colors*

*Love – pink*
*Wealth – green*
*Brain power – yellow*
*Health – blue*
*Wisdom – purple*
*Protection – white*
*Passion – red*
*Insight – silver*
*Happiness – gold*
*Luck and confidence – orange*
*Privacy – black*

### *Essential Oils*

*Communication – basil*
*Confidence – mandarin*
*Love and happiness – rose geranium*
*Spiritual strength – sandalwood*
*Protection – frankincense*
*Physical strength – lemon*
*Prosperity – bergamot*
*Sexiness – women, ylang ylang; men, cinnamon*
*Wisdom – patchouli*
*Health – lavender*

Carry a hankie scented with an appropriate essential oil
and wrapped around a crystal to charm your day.

## *Crystals*

*Empowering – clear quartz*
*Enlightening – amethyst*
*Love and friendship – rose quartz*
*Business success – jasper*
*Wisdom – bloodstone*
*Brain power – citrine*
*Communication – blue lace agate*
*Luck and courage – tiger's eye*
*Magickal power – fluorite*
*Health – women, moonstone; men, smoky quartz*

Keep a little notebook and pen in which to write any
visionary insights or arcane musings.

Write a letter to yourself at the beginning of the
week about what you hope to achieve in the coming
seven days. Place it in an envelope with a piece of
clear quartz crystal and a leaf of sage to empower, and
hide it somewhere safe to help you achieve your goals.
(After seven days, paste the letter in your Book of
Shadows and write a new one – this will keep track
of your progress and serve to inspire you further.)

Enrol in a massage or aromatherapy course, or perhaps
a nutrition or herbal medicine course. Witches are
natural healers – it's one of our greatest passions.
We know that in doing things for others we empower
ourselves. Give of yourself generously – your time
and your energy. Do some work for charity, clean up
your local park, visit a home for the elderly, cook a
super healthy dinner for your family, or just give your
loved one a surprise massage!

Take pride in yourself and always make an effort with
your appearance. As you connect with and unleash your
powers, let your magickally charged inner glow enchant
all that come in contact with you!

## THE MAGICK OF FIRE

One of the most simple and effective spells for wannabe
Witches and the professionals alike is a candle spell.
All you need is a candle in a color corresponding to your
goal, an appropriate essential oil, a sharp knife, matches,
and a few minutes in the morning or late at night.
Carve your name into one side of the candle and
your goal in the other (for example, you've had a
fight with your boyfriend and you want to make up –
for this you would carve the word "Friendship").

Lick your thumb and trace over your name with your
spit to make the candle your own. Rub a couple of
drops of essential oil into your goal (in this case you
could use rose geranium for love).

Light the candle and gaze at the flame, and see in your mind your goal manifest (in this case, you laughing and hugging your boyfriend, all memories of the argument gone). Do this for a few minutes then snuff out the candle (don't blow it out – you'd be blowing away the magick!) and put it somewhere safe.

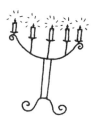

Re-lick, anoint, light, and focus on the candle for seven days or until you achieve your goal (these spells work fast as they are fuelled by the potent transformational power of fire).

## YOUR BODY IS YOUR TEMPLE —
## FEEL FREE TO RENOVATE!

Your body is your temple and just like a regular house,
sometimes it's necessary to renovate! If you are to
truly open yourself to the magick of the Universe
and unleash your secret powers then you have to have
a pure vessel as your conduit. This doesn't mean you
have to immediately become vegetarian and give up
alcohol and coffee (though if you did that would be a
terrific start!). Plenty of powerful Witches and charmed
people eat meat and enjoy a tipple – it really is about
personal choice and personal limits. This means you
need to do some soul searching, see where your diet
and lifestyle is working for you and where it isn't, and
make the appropriate adjustments.

## WHAT? NO COFFEE!

Coffee is something a lot of us take for granted – we think, "I couldn't possibly function without a cup in the morning!" Well guess what – you can. I should know, because I was one of the biggest coffee fiends around. My day started with two Italian short espressos, strong enough to strip paint! After that there were lattes, mid-morning and afternoon – on and on it went. I decided to give up coffee when I realized I was totally addicted and instead of giving me a lift, coffee had become a burden.

After a few days of feeling a bit foggy and headachy, it was like the sun emerged from behind the clouds! I started experiencing peaceful deep sleep (my insomnia totally disappeared) and I was waking in the morning feeling fresh and positive – without the coffee crutch!

The wonderful world of herbal teas then truly beckoned. I worked with herbs a lot in my Witchcraft and drank the teas, but my system was so polluted that the subtle yet far reaching effects of the herbs were totally lost on me.

I would like to suggest that you give up coffee for your magickal week to really benefit from the qualities of the suggested herbal teas. A tip for getting the most out of this is to drink with intent – being aware of the magickal folklore of the different teas – this will affect your psyche as much as the nutritional components of the herbs will affect your body and mind.

After your magickal week you may decide to give up coffee permanently – or if you enjoy the café culture (as I do!) have a decaf. Learn about the different qualities of herbal teas and vary your intake – that way you'll always be stimulated and receive the maximum benefits!

### OTHER VICES

Now to alcohol … I always considered myself a harmless "social drinker." A campari and soda at 5 p.m., a couple of glasses of wine at dinner, a nightcap of brandy later. Doesn't sound too bad, but when you do this every day of the week and add extra for some lunches and a night out it starts to add up! I realized I was starting to wake up with a hangover every day, to the extent that I thought this foggy, cloudy, slightly depressed feeling was just me being me as I got older. When I did my magickal makeover I gave up all alcohol and again the sun came out – I realized that I had been functioning well below my capabilities for a long time.

Reappraise your relationship with alcohol –
could you do with less? Would it be better enjoyed as
a sumptuous experience once a week, rather than as
an everyday habit? I absolutely adore fine wine and the
culture that surrounds it. I find I can truly appreciate
this by only drinking the very best "nectar of the sacred
vine" occasionally and for a special purpose.

Whilst I'm preaching I'll mention one more socially
condoned and advertised drug … cigarettes.
One word – urghh! If you want to breathe in smoke,
light an incense stick.

### RUBBISH-FREE FOOD

The next thing I'd like to draw your attention to is organic produce. Free-range eggs and poultry, vegetables, fruits and grains grown without pesticides, and home grown herbs nurtured with love will fuel your body with uncontaminated nutrients and super-charged life force – perfect for a practitioner of magick!

Don't feel you have to overhaul your eating overnight – even if it's just one organic apple a day it's a start on the right path. You'll find, as you refine and empower yourself, life-enhancing decisions will become second nature.

## EVERYDAY ENCHANTMENT

There are so many ways to enchant your everyday life
and the best way to start is with you and your attitude.
If you feel that, despite the modern-day emphasis on
conquering the environment and rational thought, there
is something profoundly mystical and "supernatural"
under it all, you are on the way to opening up to a
whole new reality that is enriching, inspiring, profoundly
rewarding, and truly magickal.

Here are a few simple, practical, and fun ways to start
making your home and workspace more magickal.

✳ *Try to limit the amount of toxic chemicals around you by using organic cleaning products (available at health food stores and now some supermarkets).*

✳ *To clear any stale energies and encourage harmony, add a cup of basil infusion (two handfuls of fresh leaves to a pot) to floor cleaners.*

✳ *Make an infusion of galangal and wipe it over door handles for luck.*

✳ *Hang a bunch of bay laurel over your front door to bless the house.*

✳ *Have a pot of mint growing on your work desk for better business decisions and prosperity.*

✳ *If you have a fireplace, burn lavender on the fire to protect your home and fill it with a beautiful scent.*

✳ *To bring health to your home, hang a decorative rope of garlic bulbs in the kitchen.*

✳ *To turn around bad luck, try this old Victorian method. Wear your clothes backwards or inside out! (Underwear or socks work well.)*

✳ *To further turn away bad luck add a few drops of lemongrass oil to your bath and drink lemongrass tea.*

✳ *If you see a coin on the ground, always pick it up for luck. Keep it for at least a week and then give it to charity – never spend it, that can bring bad luck.*

✳ *If it's Friday the 13th and you see a black cat, pick it up and give it a hug!*

## FINALLY...

Believe in yourself and your methods – even if others criticize you and your, perhaps newfound, awareness of Witchcraft. Criticism is usually anchored by fear of the unknown – so don't feel threatened and perhaps be prepared to educate your detractors a little! Pursue your dreams and enjoy your unique journey through the good times and the bad – a Witch embraces life in all its guises.

Remember the world answers according to the questions you ask of it. Real magick is all around you when you look for it.

Blessed Be.

**Please visit me at: www.fionahorne.com**